Poetic EMOTIONS

BK MILLS

AuthorHouse™
1663 Liberty Drive
Bloomington, IN 47403
www.authorhouse.com
Phone: 1 (833) 262-8899

Because of the dynamic nature of the Internet, any web addresses or links contained in this book may have changed since publication and may no longer be valid. The views expressed in this work are solely those of the author and do not necessarily reflect the views of the publisher, and the publisher hereby disclaims any responsibility for them.

Any people depicted in stock imagery provided by Getty Images are models, and such images are being used for illustrative purposes only.
Certain stock imagery © Getty Images.

Penciled Illustrated Art Credits;
Artist, Michelle Nicole

This book is printed on acid-free paper.

ISBN: 978-1-6655-0261-0 (sc)
ISBN: 978-1-6655-0262-7 (e)

Library of Congress Control Number: 2020919073

Print information available on the last page.

Published by AuthorHouse 10/08/2020

authorHOUSE®

The Stranger

It's amazing, how what's not liked by a close friend is well received and loved by a total stranger! It is very possible to adapt and have chemistry with a total stranger than time spent with someone for longer than a few and still not know each other. It amazes me how the more you can grow close to someone you can drift far apart at the same time. It astonishes me how you can become close to a total stranger, and are willing to spend forever getting to know them, than spend forever with someone and not know them.

1

A Friend

A Friend
A Lover
Now an Enemy;
An Enemy
A Friend
Now A Lover.

Brown Skin Girl

Brown skin girl;
Come lie next to me,
So I can be your lover,
From here to eternity.

From the top of your head;
To the souls of your feet,
Needs the touch of loving hands,
That is nothing but sweet.

Give me the chance;
I wasted before,
To prove my love,
It's worth it I'm sure.

My heart is yours; and
Your heart is mine,
So let the clouds part,
So my love can shine.

A Fantasy

Lay down besides me, and
Tell me your dreams.
While I caress your body,
With the finest of creams.

I'll unbutton your blouse, and
Unzip you're dress, and
Begin kissing your neck,
Right down to your breast.

We became closer than one;
Under the spring showers.
Where together we made love,
For more than several hours.

I massaged your back;
Right down to your feet,
While tasting your body,
Increasing the heat.

Hold me in your arms, and
Tell me what you feel.
Kiss me on my lips, and
Make sure it's for real.

True Love

I remember that precious moment;
When I first saw your beauty.
My heart beating fast,
For my future was near me.

To predict our future;
Is like telling a lie.
For a better tomorrow,
Means the start of a good day.

My love for you;
Was there at the start, but
Like an untold secret,
It was kept in my heart.

Slowly but surely;
The secret was revealed.
Like an old time mystery,
Being solved then sealed.

Step by Step;
I walked right into your life.
To better my being,
With you as my wife.

It wasn't that long ago;
When I said " I Love You " and
Thought I lied, now I realize,
Being without you is not worth living, but
Still unhappy if I died.

Every-time I see you;
I see an angel sent from above, and
Anytime you're near or besides me,
I become a fool who's fallen deeper and deeper in love.

We laid down as friends, and
Woke up as lovers.
That's a dream that many wish true, but
I'm the fortunate one that,
Experienced my real and true Love with you!

I Love You!

Everlasting Love

The sun shines light;
Across the land.

With you in my sight, and
Your life in my hand.

The love we share;
Is shared by two.

With all my heart,
I'll always love you!

The feel of your love;
Circles around me, and

The warmth of your kiss,
Is within me.

My soul is at rest;
Lifted high above.

From ones sweet caress,
I'm a fool for your love.

Between you and I;
The secret is open.

Caught with one eye,
My love is unspoken.

A Quiet Love

The night is young;
Where love has grown.
A love so strong,
It can't be wrong.
The whispers at night;
Only I can hear.
Silently flow to my ear.
Your body held close and tight;
Stirred with emotions,
That feel so right.
In my arms you fall asleep;
As my thoughts drift higher above.
Quietly inside I began to weep,
Because I've fallen deeper and deeper in love.

Love

Love brings such joy;
To the heart,
Of all life's pleasures;
Loves the sweetest part.

Love is like a gentle breeze;
Blowing through the night,
My mind is calm and set at ease;
Filled with passion and delight.

The thought is strong, but
Yet so near.
It feels as though,
I'm close to there.

My time will come;
So still I wait.
For the love of mine,
To share and mate.

The feel of your love;
Is sweet and pure.
When times for love,
You'll know for sure.

It's a wonderful thing;
To be in love,
To feel your heart beat fast.
It's a wonderful time to be in love,
When it's finally here at last.

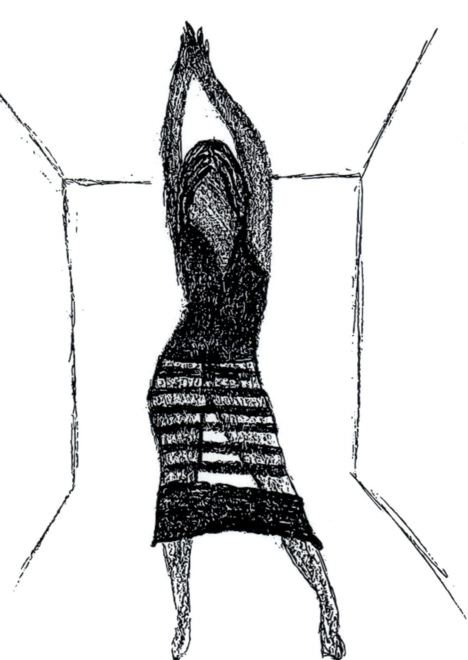

Center Of Attraction

Amongst the crowd,
You've become the center of attraction.

Before the eyes of many,
You're the one that stood out.

I made my way over, and
Asked for your hand.

We shared a romantic dance, and
Some lovin' at nights end.

Am I wrong for what I've done,
Or right in a sense.

Forgive me my lady;
For I fall for those,
Who are the center of attraction.

Red Rose

In the midst of the cornfield;
Stands this one rose.
That rose is you,
The love I've been searching for.

Thru the hot summer days; and
Cold winter nights.
Your desire to grow,
Did not burn out.

Noticed by many;
Thought by few.
Am I the only one,
That's in love with you.

Give me the chance;
To carry you home.
Grow you in my heart,
To keep forever as my own.

Poison

Do not call out for me;
For I am poison.

Do not reach for my hand;
For I am poison.

Do not wish to embrace me;
For I am poison.

Do not attempt to kiss me;
For I am poison.

Do not try and make love to me;
For I am poison.

There once was a time;
I called out out for you.
You were poison!

There once was a time;
I reached out for you.
You were poison!

There once was a time;
I was in need for warm
embrace.
You were poison!

There once was a time;
I tried to kiss you.
You were poison!

There once was a time;
I tried to make love to you.
You were poison!

I heard, you didn't listen;
We were poison!

I looked, you didn't see;
We were poison!

I touched, you didn't feel;
We were poison!

I talked, you didn't speak;
We were poison!

I licked, and you tasted;
Because we knew it was poison!

A Dream

I wish as we walk side by side,
Holding each other's hand;
On the white sands of the most beautiful beach.

As the warm water of the deep blue ocean;
Creeps up on shore and meets our feet,
We stop, and stand still, and gaze at the dark skies.

As the moon and the stars shed light before our faces;
A dream begins.
Between us both,
It's a dream hidden deep within.

Just as night appears, day begins and the dream is over.

A Kiss

Pretty as a rose, and
The sexiest of red.
You're the one my heart has chose,
To lay forever in my bed.

Constantly a thought in my mind;
You're the one I'll always love.
With you, my past is left behind,
Thanks to great man up above.

Fulfill my every fantasy, and
My one and every wish.
Quench my desire, by
Sealing it with a kiss.

If I

If I was blind,
You're beauty is all I see.

If I was deaf,
Your voice is all I hear.

If I was mute,
I'll try and say " I Love You"

If I was cripple,
I'll find a way to reach you.

If all I feel is sadness,
Your comfort makes me happy.

If all I feel is hate,
With you I'll always love.

If I had one question,
You would be the answer.

If I had no choice but death,
You're the reason why I live.

Sins Of Desire

I want to hold, kiss, and
Suck on your lips, and
Stroke that sexy body,
Till I reach those hips.

I'll lay you on your back;
As you yearn for more.
Of the sinful desire,
That I kept in store.

Licking on your neck;
Chests, and Thigh, and the
The sucking on your tongue,
That bares truth and no lie.

Honey on your breast;
Makes lovin' more sweet.
As I lick, lick, lick,
What's my favorite treat.

Baby, I want you;
More than before.
Don't keep me waiting,
It's worth it for sure.

Summer

Summer, Summer, what a beautiful season,
Why you may ask there's no number one reason.

Perhaps it's the white sands on Caribbean Beaches,
Or the sweet luscious fruit that a tree unleashes.

Perhaps it's the sweat that's worked up at night,
From the making of love that seems to be right.

Perhaps the short strolls that led to long walks,
Or the swims at nights and the heavy love talks.

Perhaps it's the four-play under the moonlight,
Or the thoughts in mind that's kept inside tight.

Perhaps if Summer was a woman,
How would I feel.
Just to hold Summers hands, and
Kiss Summers lips.

Perhaps it's a fantasy,
Or possibly a dream.
Could it come true,
That remains to be seen.

So, if anyone asks?
Why Summer is a beautiful season?
You'll have to ask the woman,
Or else there's no number one reason!

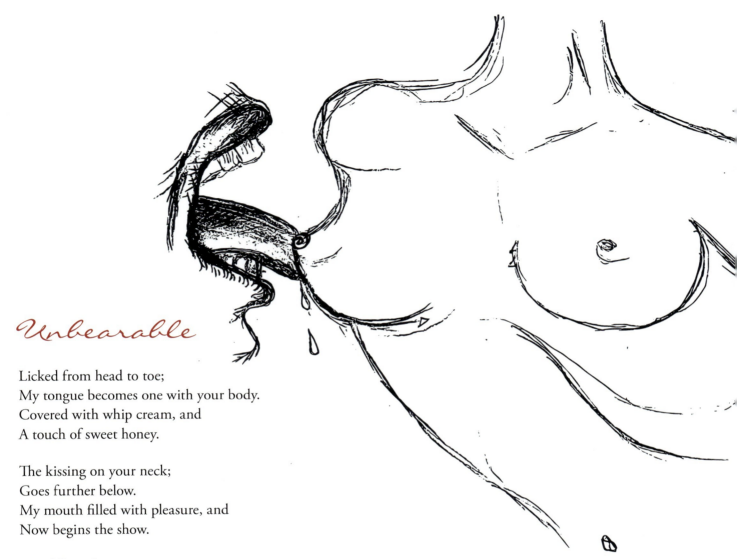

Unbearable

Licked from head to toe;
My tongue becomes one with your body.
Covered with whip cream, and
A touch of sweet honey.

The kissing on your neck;
Goes further below.
My mouth filled with pleasure, and
Now begins the show.

As I follow the sweat;
That flows down south.
I begin to satisfy and devour,
With the lips on my mouth.

The moaning and groaning;
Becomes music to my ear.
Because of the sweet love making,
That few can bare.

My Desire

Friendly conversations and wise advise,
Are often shared between us.
Secrets as well as honest promises,
Are stored deep within.

My desire and feelings for you,
Has reached another level.
No longer a friend in my eyes,
But a lover in my heart.

When I look deep into your eyes,
The thought of kissing you crosses my mind.
Why can't we lay down as friends, and
Wake up as lovers?

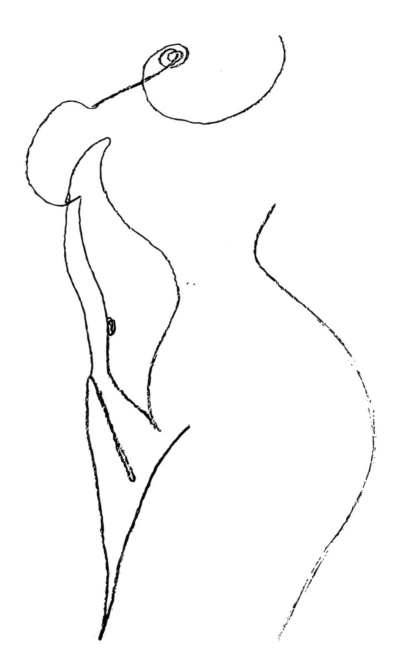

My Season

My heart beats like the loudest of;
Thunders and pouring rain.
My desires streaks thru my veins, like
Lightening in the night skies.

My want of you is;
Like the Summer heat.
Yet only recently became,
Like the Winter cold.

Beautiful and pure like;
The whitest of snow,
And the most beautiful of flowers that,
blossoms in the Spring.

Sensual as Autumn colors; and
Leaves in the Fall.
You stand before me,
The rarest season of all.

I'll Be

I'll be the bed that lies beneath your body, and
The pillow that's beneath your head.

I'll be the comforter that comforts you at night, and
The lover that's always by your side.

I'll be the shoulders your problems rest upon, and
The ears that listens to your worries.

I'll be those warm hands that massages your back, and
Those kisses that quenches your thirst.

I'll be the chocolate that melts in your mouth, and
The strawberries that bringeth sweet taste.

I'll be the rain that falls upon you, and
The towel that dries every drop.

I'll be the winds that blows thru your hair, and
The mists that cools your body down.

I'll be your everything from beginning to end,
Even if that means just being a friend.

Live Free

Burdens and worries,
Weighs on my shoulders like a ton.
As thoughts in my head,
Prevent me from moving on.

Memories and past times,
Keeps me from seeing ahead.
As I load bullet after bullet,
Contemplating the chrome to my head.

It all crosses our mind,
Every now and then.
Throwing our hands to the heavens,
Hoping for it all to end.

You see, we all live the same,
Balancing life the best we could.
Trying to live a decent life,
The best way we should.

Our bodies are temporary,
But the Spirit caged within is everlasting.
Once the outer layer is shed,
The life within you will freely sing.

By Your Side

Focus on the good; and
Don't even think about the bad.
Forgive and forget the past,
Push forward and better your future.

There is no challenge; that
You cannot handle, because
The more you try,
The more you'll truly succeed.

Open your eyes; and
See what I see.
Always expecting the worse, and
Faithfully Hoping for the best.

I'm here for you;
Thru thick and thin.
When you think you're alone,
I'm right here by your side.

Only Time Will Tell

I received a call;
In the middle of the night.
"Honey be ready"
"I'm passing by tonight"

My heart beating fast;
As I wait to submit.
In the darkest room,
Where candles are lit.

Satin sheets;
Remains to be ruffled.
From the two bodies that
Maketh sweet love.

Is it worth the wait?
Or a waste of my time!
I'll tell in the morn'
Cause now is my time!

Bed Of Roses

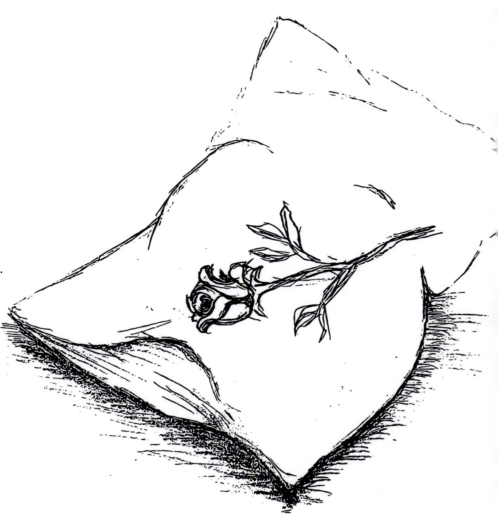

On a bed of roses;
Lies your caramel like body.
Melting away under satin sheets,
Awaiting ones answer to your fantasy.

Your fantasy;
Is my desire to share with you.
Your dreams,
Are my wishes we both can make true.

Your desires and wants;
Are the same on my list.
Starting with the look in your eyes,
Ending with that long awaited kiss.

The nature of your beauty;
Was sent from above.
A purpose in which was not served,
Until together we make love.

No, is not an answer;
Yes, is not just to say.
Give me a chance,
While we become one, as we lay.

Poetry In Motion

When I look at you,
One thought crosses my mind.
What the feeling would be,
Entering you from behind.

Pushing your head forward,
Breathing on the back of your neck.
Caressing your body,
Poetry in Motion on deck.

The oceans affect,
From the hidden caves within.
Drives the inner spirit wild,
Engaging in passionate sin.

Like the stroke of a poets pen;
Or the direction from the painters brush.
At the height of ecstasy,
Your warm waters begin to rush.

The shivers and quivers;
Runs down our spine.
As together you and I,
Make love that's Divine.

Our souls collide; and
Our spirits connect.
As our bodies unite,
Poetry in Motion on deck.

Passion and Desire;
Is the look in our eyes.
As the Poetry in Motion,
Occurs between your thighs.

Hmmmm, those teardrops;
That streamed from your eyes.
From the Poetry In Motion,
That ex lovers despise.

Our bodies produce;
The most sensual love potion.
As our temperatures rise,
Thrusting with the deepest of emotion.

Passionate words penned;
Was the finest of the Kings Notion.
As the King lays with his Queen,
Making Love Poetry In Motion.

There Is Nothing Like

There is nothing like;
Seeing you slip out of your heels.
Reaching for a bottle of wine, and
Getting all up in your feels.

There is nothing like;
Letting your hair all down.
From a long day at work,
Laying in that see thru gown.

There is nothing like;
The perfume scent that you wear.
As the aroma is euphoric,
The closer your body gets near.

There is nothing like;
That noise that you make.
Laying there on your back,

For the Love of God sake.

There is nothing like;
Doing anything you please.
There is nothing like,
The way you fall to your knees.

There is nothing like;
Parting your deep seas.
There is nothin like,
Your bare essential tease.

There is nothing like;
Laying with you through the night.
No, there is nothing like,
Your bare assets that's in sight.

Nope, there is nothing like.......

Last Night

Walking side by side;
With someone else on my mind,
Trying to seem interested, carefully
Not getting into a bind.

We walk and talk; and her voice;
Is the only one I hear.
Even though your right in front of me,
She's the one that's standing there.

When asked about "that look";
I quickly brushed it off.
Reassuring her all is good,
Clutching her hand ever so soft.

Later on that night,
Sitting near the fireplace.
You sat besides me, and
Looked into my face.

I saw your lips moving; but
Didn't hear one word that was said.
She said I cannot compete,
With whomever is in my head.

As the night carried on;
She found your strand in my bed,
But didn't say a word,
Knowing what lies ahead.

Not realizing that;
I was in clear and present danger.
Holding up your strand, asking
If you're a friend or total stranger.

My response wasn't clear;
Not sure what I even said.
I just couldn't let her know, that
Last night you were in my bed.

Masterpiece

There is a masterpiece;
That's in the corner of the room.
Gazing out the window,
Staring at the flowers as they bloom.

Butterflies gracefully fly through the air;
As birds chirp top the nearby trees.
Sounds of the morning air, gently
Blowing by calmly at ease.

Torn at the corners;
Wearing a broken heart.
There is a masterpiece,
A wonderful work of art.

Staring there looking out the window;
Watching the sun rise in the east.
Standing there in all her beauty,
There is a masterpiece.

Angel From Above

In my eyes, you're the beauty;
That was sent from above.

Despite what I think or say;
You're the woman I have grown to love.

The looks in your eyes;
Shows me how much you really care.

However, I failed to realize it;
Because it's a feeling that's truly rare.

The obvious goes mostly unseen;
Because a fool is often blinded by love.

If there is one thing I can say or do;
Is to treat you like an angel from above.

Becoming One

I know I told you,
You'll never hear from me ever again.
Words that I definitely regret,
From the words written from my pen.

It was said out of anger,
Your words cut to the core.
The more the days go by,
I want you more and more and more.

I think you already know,
If you and I lock eyes.
That the feelings held inside,
Will lead to those moans and sighs.

There is something about your warmth,
Throughout your hidden tavern.
Becoming one on Satin sheets,
Next to the dim lit lantern.

No words can describe,
What my inner soul speaks.
Reaching out for your desire,
From the hills and mountain peaks.

Like a ball player becomes,
One with their cleats.
You remember how we became one,
those nights in the sheets.

Time has gone by, and
The wound will not heal.
Until you and I,
Make love that is real.

Sealed With A Kiss

The envelope was just sealed;
Penned emotions contained inside.
Placed in a box for a later date,
Was the feelings kept bottled up inside.

It reads,

My apologies to you;
My beautiful lady.
For portraying a little boy,
When it was a man I was suppose to be.

Forgive me;
For not really knowing what to do.
Looking deep into your eyes, and
Expressing my deep emotions for you.

If the answer is no;
I have one last wish.
That you say yes,
Sealing it with a kiss.

Marry Me

Your eyes are the lights;
That brightens up my world, and
Your beauty leaves me speechless,
Far beyond any other girl.

I love you very much;
Is a statement that reads true, and
The statement that's said next,
Are those sweet words I do.

There's a well know secret;
That's locked up in my heart, and
The key that opens it was,
You from the very start.

Listen to these words;
For it will make me happy, and
Respond with the right answer,
That you will be mine and Marry Me?

What Is Real

Kiss me,
Not once but twice;
So I know the first was real.

Hug me,
Not once but twice;
So I know the first was real.

Make love to me,
Not once but twice;
So I know the first was real.

Be my lady,
Just once, not twice;
Cause I know the first is real.

What They Seem

What if life is just a dream, and
Nothing seen thru ones eyes
Is what they seem.

What if this is the afterlife, and
The pains, anguish, and strife is
Exactly what they seem.

One can only wonder, why?
All we know is absolutely nothing,
Because nothing is what they seem!

Tell Me The Truth

You want me to fall in love with you?
Drop the makeup and show me your pain.
Don't put up a facade or show,
That lost will provide you no gain.

You judge me, because of things I say;
Even casted me out of your congregation.
When spoken of, nothing good is said,
Spreading false news amongst the nation.

Tears streaming with raw emotion;
As my voice whispers from the hurt and pain.
I been there, done that, maybe twice;
Yet still managed not to go insane.

I don't wear my emotions on my sleeve;
Often I won't say, how I really feel.
I mean c'mon who is really listening,
We all have issues you know the deal.

Nothing I do is good for you;
Yet continue to talk having nothing to say;
Often criticizing me behind my back,
Simply because I don't do it your way.

How hard is it to really live a simple life?
With all the fussin' and fighting that goes on.
It's only the two of us behind closed doors, and
Yet we still argue who's right and who's wrong.

It's a choice to make it work;
All we have to do is try.
Are you willing if I'm able?
Tell me the truth and don't lie.

Truth Or Dare

My lover is far over seas, but
The love I want is close and near.
I thought I was in love,
Now I'm facing fear.
On a decision that's based on
Truth or Dare!

Open Eyes

If I knew, what I know now;
I wouldn't even try.
Now, that reality looks me in the face,
I'll stop living this lie.

I was living a dream;
That was too good to be true.
Now, my eyes are open, and
I am a fool for you.

Regrets for all I caused you;
From the bottom of my heart, but
You wouldn't listen,
Even from the very start.

You're to much for me to handle;
Even with given strength from above, but
My eyes still set on you,
I'll just never know if it was love.

I Am Your Soul

I've poured out my heart and soul;
Into your broken cup. As you stand,
There wondering where my love has gone,
While holding the broken cup.

She cries, she hurts, she pains;
She heard it all before.
She gave her heart and her soul,
And still gives a lil more.

During the day she smiles;
At night she's sad and cries.
No one can imagine her pain,
At night inside slowly she dies.

In her eyes I see her past;
In her voice I feel her break.
She walks alone and talks aloud,
Imagining how much more she can take.

For years she spoke and had no voice;
Saddened and broken from her past.
Decisions and consequences lurk behind,
Until that day finally came at last.

He said, I have been watching you;
Broken yet still able to smile.
You come from a broken past,
Yet you continue forward all the while.

Your heart is held by the last vein;
Pumping what's left feeding your soul.
Inside you weep and cry in pain,
Trying to become sane and become whole.

In your pain, I see a treasure;
Worth more than silver and gold.
The rarest of all wines placed on the shelf,
Getting better with age as it gets old.

You're that gem that sparkles the brightest;
When held and properly shined.
Like a needle found in the haystack,
You're the rarest gem of its kind.

Tears ran down her face;
As she heard these words spoken.
She couldn't believe that he was,
The only one that knew she was broken.

He said I am your soul,
That is why I understand your pain.
I followed besides you,
Even in the pouring rain.

You didn't recognize me;
But I was there the whole time.
Never left your side ever,
Was always just one step behind.

As far as the shadow can cast;
I was there by your side.
But you didn't recognize me,
I was there the whole ride.

Now that you see; and
Recognize that it's me.
Can we finally go home, and
Live the live we were meant to be.

One Last Chance?

I remember when I first saw you,
I took notice at first glance.....
Thought about you for a few,
Until I saw you that second chance.

There is so much beauty in your imperfection,
And yes, you're that diamond in a rough.....
The finest wine in the selection,
Not being able to taste you is definitely tough.

It all started with a simple "Hello",
And ended with a painful "Goodbye".....
They say opposites attract, maybe, I guess, or simply don't know.....
But, you're the apple in the center of my eye.

In such a short period of time,
I knew that you were rare.....
And I dropped it like one drops a dime,
Wondering around with that dazed stare.

I don't know what else to say,
And I know you understand.....
That I'm hopeful for the day,
Where you'll reach out and grab my hand.

Everything I told you, was from my heart,
I never once lied to you.....
Not even from the very start,
When I told you, that I Love you.

I'm sorry for not being a friend,
Sorry for walking away from our dance.....
Sorry for not being understanding from beginning
to end.....
And I'm asking for one last chance?

It is very, very, rare;
To have the type of chemistry once shared.
I knew there was something special, at the very first
stare;
As well as feelings that I very much feared.

You see, the truth is I actually care;
And I didn't see it coming at all,
This game of life, love, truth, and dare;
Is the reason why great men fall.

You're a constant thought in mind;
That I can't shake no matter how much I try.
You're the right dose of crazy of it's kind;
That I need in my life, I tell you no lie.

At first, I knew you wouldn't give me the time of day.
And in our short period of time;

You have been the one that got away.
Despite it being surreal and sublime.
At times I reach deep;
To find the right words.
Some I definitely decide to keep;
So I don't strike the wrong chords.

I definitely want another chance;
Even if it means being a friend.
It's like carrying the sword to a dance;
And I know you will hurt me in the very end.

Yet, despite the way you feel for me;
I rather have you for a day.
Because the only thing I see;
Is for you to give in and say ok.

I shouldn't be feeling this way;
And I can't help but express them to you.
At one point we spoke all times of the day;
Now I'm here wondering what's left to do.

I hate saying I'm sorry;
Because it's just an excuse to do it again.
Even if someone else makes you happy; I'll rather not
hear about it, and just be a good friend.

Please, think about it and give me an opportunity;
Give me a second chance to do it again.
No need too rush, or do anything hastily;
I'll just wait patiently till the end.

Second Chance At Romance

You had the chance,
To grab hold of my hand.
However, you let go, and
Now you don't understand.

It was good while it lasted, but
Abruptly came to an end.
With no given explanation,
I lost a genuine friend.

I didn't see it coming,
As you know I was blindsided.
I respect your decision, but
That convo was one sided.

I took it on the chin,
With a grain of salt.
Listening in utter shock,
As everything came to a halt.

In utter disbelief.
I got up and walked away.
Having nothing to say,
Even to this very day.

Time has passed by,
With you still on my mind.
Wondering what would have been,
If you didn't leave me far behind.

Now it seems you want,
What we already had.
Realizing everything was all good, and
Our past wasn't at all bad.

They say distance makes,
The heart grow fond.
Hopefully this saying is true,
So we could rekindle our bond.

I am willing if you are able,
To give it another chance.
No need for lengthy discussions,
Just a second chance at romance.

I told you how special and rare you are,
From the very start, and
Yes when I said "I Love You"
It was truly from the bottom of my heart.

Footprints

I chased the footprints;

On the winters white snow,

Footsteps that climbed out of my heart;

And into the open.

Beyond the trees; and

Cast of shadows,

Are those lovely footprints;

That I long to follow.

Faded Memories

As the sunlight glistens, across the ocean,
There's a sudden calm in the breeze.
Bright hues in the summer skies,
Comforting the birds, and the sweet honey bees.

As the sun sets behind the horizon,
The sounds of crashing waves roar.
Washing away our footprints,
As waters creep up further upon shore.

Memories like footprints in the sand;
Quickly disappear as fast as I look.
As if, they never were there,
Fading away as my head shook.

Watching the sailboat sail away,
As it vanishes amongst the seas.
Is how life seems to be,
Walking the beach, hand in hand,
With Faded Memories.

The Run Away

You can't want Love, and

Then Run away.

Then Fall in Love, and

Run away.

In Love or not,

You'll always be,

The one, that will

Always Run Away.

On The Run

You know it ain't easy being me;
I go thru the struggles of life too.
You once was that ear that would listen,
Even if you didn't really want to.

It's good to be alone;
No one else to place the blame.
Thats why life is the way it is, but
With you it wasn't the same.

There comes a point in your life;
When you really want to get it right.
Tired of messing things up,
Destroying everything in sight.

Friends and Family may never understand;
Why you got the very best of me.
It only takes that special one,
For all to see that reality.

Your own friends will despise you;
Your own family will puff and pout.
That's the irony of the life we live,
I just needed time to figure it all out.

Everyone thinks they know what's good for you;
They bought into all the system has to offer them.
Been told your going to hell,
Just because you won't mingle with em'

We all need to breathe; and
Spread our wings and fly.
Leaving the struggles and worries, but
All we can do is painfully cry.

From the scars of ones past;
You hear the beauty in ones voice.
Raw emotions and passion,
From things that left her no choice.

If you only really knew;
How I have eyes for no one but you, and
How my spirit would become alive,
When we would do what we do.

Our hearts are both broken;
Together our pieces become one.
My inner soul trembles and yearns,
Ever since you've been on the run.

Woman Of Sin

Why am I attracted to Delilah,
Cause she'll cut my hair, and
Gauge my eyes out.
I'm attracted to the woman of sin!

Why am I attracted to Eve,
Cause she'll make me take a bite,
Of her forbidden fruit,
I'm attracted to the woman of sin.

Why am I attracted to Jezebel,
Cause she'll make love to me, and
Break my heart,
I'm attracted to the woman of sin.

Why am I attracted to Tamar,
Cause she was on the side of the road
Behind the veil, Appearing appealing,
I'm attracted to the woman of sin.

Why am I attracted to Rahab, the
Harlot who lied to the king.
Because she saved the household,
I'm attracted to the woman of sin.

The list can go on and on,
As there is something appealing.
In all that's wrong within her,
I'm attracted to the woman of sin.

Wishing You Were Besides Me

I toss and turn,

Each and every night,

Vivid images of you In my head,

As I lay on my pillow.

Wishing you were besides me,

Like the good ole' days,

Where we lay together,

With no care in the world.

A wish, turns into a dream,

A dream, turns into a vision,

A vision, turns into a nightmare,

A nightmare, became reality.

Laying here wishing,

You were besides me.

Tempted

I'm tempted to touch;
Tempted to reach out, but
I won't.

I'm tempted to call;
Tempted to reach out, but
I won't.

I'm tempted to pass by;
Tempted to reach out, but
I won't.

I'm tempted to embrace you;
Tempted to reach out, but
I won't.

I'm tempted to kiss you;
Tempted to reach out, but
I won't.

I'm tempted to make love to you;
Tempted to reach out, but
I won't.

If you are tempted to reach out;
Reach out, but
I won't.

The First Time When It Was Felt

Its killing me, deep down inside,
As I scroll through the memories.
Remembering the good times we had,
No longer friends but distant enemies.

It pierces deep down to the soul,
It cuts down deep to the bone.
You'll always have a piece of my heart,
Despite your heart being cold as stone.

I know there is no words, and
I'm running out of things to say.
The task is difficult moving on,
As you cross my mind every single day.

Oh, how I wish to hold you,
Running my fingers through your hair.
Gazing thru your eyes,
Falling in love with your simple stare.

As the days turn to nights,
I toss forever in my bed.
Desires for you running wild,
As vivid images flows through my head.

The kisses that we shared, was
The sweetest of its kind, and
Your sensual, warm embrace, was
As rare as any one can possibly find.

Time will pass by, and
I will wither and grow old.
But, I'll never forget,
The short love story we told.

At times I do regret,
That day I asked for your name.
Wishing nothing had ever started,
Playing this dangerous love game.

It was good while it lasted,
I'm pretty sure you taste the same.
Yes, I remember all your spots,
I too was there when we played that game.

Body temperatures would rise,
Our connected bodies would melt.
You remember that feeling, the
First time When it was felt.

You Were Gone

When I opened my eyes you were gone;
Leaving no trace in sight.
Pacing back and forth;
Containing my emotions with all my might.

As I reminisce, about the times we had;
My spirit becomes free.
At times bringing a smile to my face,
A smile that very few can see.

Thinking about the good times;
That you and I both shared.
They were priceless and precious moments,
As I gently stroke the gray in my beard.

Yesterday is a pastime;
Today will come and go.
Tomorrow isn't promised,
This much I know.

Physically here, but mentally there;
It's a tough act to put on.
Like, I said before,
When I opened my eyes,
You were gone.

I Had A Dream

I remember very clearly;
That time when I gave up.
Asking the heavens for a sign,
Because so much had filleth my cup.

One night I had a dream;
Remember it like yesterday.
A feeling never felt before,
Until the day you came my way.

It was just an aura;
Of pure shear beauty.
The closer I drew near,
Wild passion burns with fire and intensity.

You had no face;
Yet I knew you were beautiful.
You were just a vague silhouette,
Yet your nature kept me full.

It wasn't until that day;
As I was just sitting there, when
A feeling so soulfully strong,
Allowed the dream to became more clear.

It was you, the dream had shown;
I knew when that feeling appeared,
Crippling me to my knees,
Revealing everything I feared.

You are the one;
That appeared with no face.
You are that silhouette,
That stood there in place.

You are that aura;
That was that mysterious beauty.
You are the one,
My dream has prepared for me.

Wherever

Whether it's in the States;
Or out of the Country.
Wherever you are at,
That's where I will be.

Whether it's in the big City;
Or Third World Country.
Wherever you are at,
That's where I will be.

Whether it's in the Loft;
Or Middle of some unknown Country.
Wherever you are at,
That's where I will be.

Basically, what I'm saying;
No matter where you will be.
Wherever you are at,
That's where I will be.

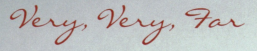

Very, Very, Far

You can't bring the stars in;
Any closer than they are.
No matter where you stand,
They're still very, very, far.

Standing there besides me;
We look at the same star.
Together we may stand,
They're still very, very, far.

No longer there besides me;
We gaze at the same star.
Standing in between two lands,
They're still very, very, far.

From wherever we are;
We see the same star.
No matter where we stand,
We're not very, very, far.

As we look;
At the very same star.
No matter where we stand,
We're not very, very, far.

You Were The One

Had many women in my life;
None stuck out more than you.
Yes, it's true; one time I had a wife,
Maybe you and I should have said "I do"

There's levels to this game of love;
That many of us take for granted.
When push comes to shove,
You were the one that I truly wanted.

Didn't care that you wasn't perfect;
Neither am I, tell you the truth.
Had no idea you would have this affect,
Like my first crush when I was a youth.

At least I can say I had a taste;
From the juice of your sweet honeydew.
Memories that will never go to waste,
Especially the ones making love to you.

I always worked up a sweat;
Those hot and steamy nights, and
you were a little bit more than wet,
As you climaxed to soulful heights.

You use to love as I growled in your ear;
Clutching tightly the small of your back.
Burying your face in the length of your hair
Exploring every nook, cranny, and crack.

There's a few that got away;
A few I didn't care to lose.
I knew from that very day,
You were the one I forever choose.

Passionate Sin

You're one of the wonders;
Not counted in the seven.
Beautiful and perfectly crafted,
With hints and remnants of heaven.

Her scent is simply amazing;
Smile more radiant than sunshine.
Skin soft to the touch, as
Fingers trickle down her spine.

Hair wavier than the bluest ocean;
Voice smoother than calm wind.
Breaking each and every rule,
As we lay committing passionate sin.

Even an angel would be enticed;
Willing to lose its wings.
For a night of sensual pleasures,
Engaged in passionate sin.

The angel will lose its luster;
Chasing the chase to the win.
Willing to become human,
Engaging in passionate sin.

Hostage

Stuck and trapped from my past;
I can never seem to move on.
In my head, mind, body, and soul,
It squeezes my being till I am no more.
Appearing heartless and cold;
Losing a grip at times.
Trapped from images in my head, and
The thoughts seen in my mind.
Bound and gagged like a savage;
Beaten and thrown to the curb.
Left for dead, for vultures and wolves,
In my mind I'm holding myself hostage.

Freeing yourself is a task;
Living life in constant bondage.
In my mind I'm left alone,
Trapped and held hostage.
Just riding around thinking;
About you all the time.
Making it worse on myself,
Feeling like I committed a crime.
Wishing you'd return packed; and
Sealed with the rarest postage.
For now return to sender it says,
Or is that me holding myself hostage.

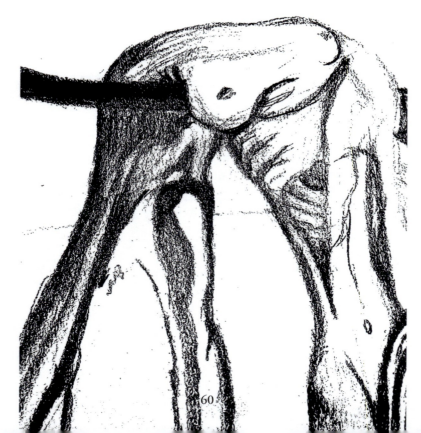

Love Stains

Moon lit and star-bright nights;
Candles lit, music low, and satin sheets.
Grandfather clock striking midnight, as
You enter the door, looking like the finest of treats.

Trailing you with my eyes;
As you walk across the room.
As your aroma follows behind,
From the scent of your perfume.

Sex on the beach incense;
Burns through the air.
As I unzip your blouse, whispering
Poetic Emotions into your ear.

Tilting your head forward;
Unzipping you with my teeth.

Embracing you from behind,
Temperatures rise from the heat.

Aroused from your touch;
Being kissed ever so gently.
Tasting your exotic flavors,
As love stains run free.

Love stains the heart;
The quicker it beats.
It runs down our souls, but tonight
Love stains the sheets.

Love stains in the middle;
Of the night, Love stains
Between two that's intertwined,
Love stains the sheets tonight.

Let It Go

It's easy for one to say;
Drop it and let it go.
Till it happens to them,
Then they'll really know.
Heart no longer full;
Beaten and Flattened.
From all the that life gives, thinking
How could this have happened.
Some may never see;
Some will never know.
The tears flow from the pain.
Simply because I just won't let it go.

Walked Away

You can never heal her soul;
Once it has been broken.
Scarred from her past,
Hidden secrets never spoken.

Even though she smiles;
She's in a lot of pain.
Pushing forward regardless,
Trying to maintain.

Her pain also hidden;
Deep within her eyes.
From all the inner bruises,
Broken promises and Lies.

She knows he loves her;
Yet it wasn't enough.
So, he walked away,
Even though it was tough.

Before Time Began

Imagine, total darkness in the abyss; before any of the elements that occupies space was placed. Before the formations of what is called the universe occurred. That total darkness.......where any light could have been seen, despite the infinite space and darkness in the abyss.

Imagine a peace, in the quiet, darkness. Where freely one can roam in the eternal realm of the abyss, yet never known or visible. Imagine the existence before existence began, imagine life before life began. How tranquil, how serene, how beautiful is the undisturbed darkness, despite its appearance in the abyss.

Imagine a beautiful mind bringing into existence by simple thought, elements unknown from its origins to man. Elements that sustains man despite mans existence ever becoming known.

Imagine the day before day began since time is an element of the day. Before the elements placed to separate the day and the night. There once was a day before time began.

The darkness knew the light existed, and knew when it was present, even though it was never shown. Suddenly the light, was shown and revealed the power of the mind. Before darkness was formed, the light always was known.

If the light was not shown, would all we know not exists? Would it not be revealed that such a mystery exists? Would the darkness acknowledge it's existence before the light was revealed?

If the darkness was beautiful, undisturbed. Did the light instigate the mystery's unknown? Did the light reveal too much when in the abyss and the darkness was shown? Did the darkness know it contained mysteries that were hidden until it was revealed? Did the light know the darkness would react?

There once was a day before time began and it was beautiful! There once was a time before time was known where the existence of the darkness was peaceful.

Life in essence is beautiful as the light. But death is peaceful in the abyss with no revelations in sight. The existence of the eternal realm, within the abyss of the peaceful darkness, is when our eyes are closed. Eyes open doesn't necessarily mean everything will be seen, but when the eyes close, everything that's truth is exactly how it seems!

Understand

I just don't understand;
Why we choose not to get along.
It doesn't matter how we look,
Just how we right the wrong.

You and I are simply the same;
Passing thru for simply a day.
Continually playing these foolish games,
Till all is gone with nothing to say.

Mothers against daughters;
Fathers against sons.
Neighbor against neighbor,
Brandishing their guns.

Leave it up to man;
To lead us all astray.
While humanity is suffering,
Every single day.

One day we'll get it right; but
Would it be to late.
Because we just don't understand,
That we can't replace what we didn't create.

Don't Cry

Don't cry, before the beginning began,
The last day was seen and it was good.
From the beginning of time,
Man has destroyed the worlds mood.

Loving and hating one another,
Killing and raping mothers and daughters.
Shooting and stabbing each other,
Drowning fathers and sons in bloody waters.

Mankind cries out yet no one is heard,
Mother Earth is also crying out.
Yet wakes and funerals pile up,
As loved ones cry out and shout.

Boundaries drawn amongst the free land,
Controlled by the power of the Prince.
We came a long way since the beginning,
But it's been this way ever since.

Feed your brother, clothe your sister; and
Never turn your back on mom and dad.
For your days will be numbered, calling
Bad things good and good things bad.

The world is crying out from its knees,
A world stretched thin and stressed.
Not everyone can handle it well, but
The secret is knowing we all are Blessed.

Until the last day finally arrives;
It's ok to hurt and cry.
Trust me the day is at hand,
Faithfully Trusting in The Most High.

It Will All Be Over

The moon shines brightly;
Across the rainforest.
Quickly covered by clouds,
Like the way your heart is for me.

Cold and hardened;
Like the rain in the fall.
Your feelings have become,
Hidden in the grass that stands tall.

Alone in the dark;
She cries In her house.
As mascara runs from her,
Cheek right down to her blouse.

Broken, in pain and screaming;
All that's left in her being.
Scarred and broken-hearted,
Kept from everyone seeing.

Hesitant to give her heart;
Quickly pulling and running away.
Heading in the other direction,
Making everyone get out the way.

Your Love is too good;
As cliché to be true.
I'm broken and damaged,
What good am I to you.

Your kiss although beautiful;
Reminds me of those days.

Your touch and sensual desire,
Yes, it does make me feel a way.

I'm one wrong move from my;
heart to completely break.
I'm sorry but I can't commit,
This is all my heart can take.

Tears stream down my face;
Having no words to reply.
To the truth she just said,
Honestly spoken with no lie.

Now that I realize;
All that was said.
It will all be over,
The minute I open my eyes.

Like a moth to a flame;
That can't stay away.
It will all be over,
The very next Day.

Time Is Not On Your Side

Time is never on your side;
When you're looking at the clock.
Even when the clock stops working,
Time is never on your side.
In one full day;
You can accomplish a lot.
In ones lifetime,
Time is never on your side.
We burn every bridge;

Without even crossing it.
When you had the time to cross,
Time is never on your side.
How can time, time out?
If time is never on your side.
Stop Looking at the clock;
Cause when the clock,
Strikes your last hour,
Time is never on your side.

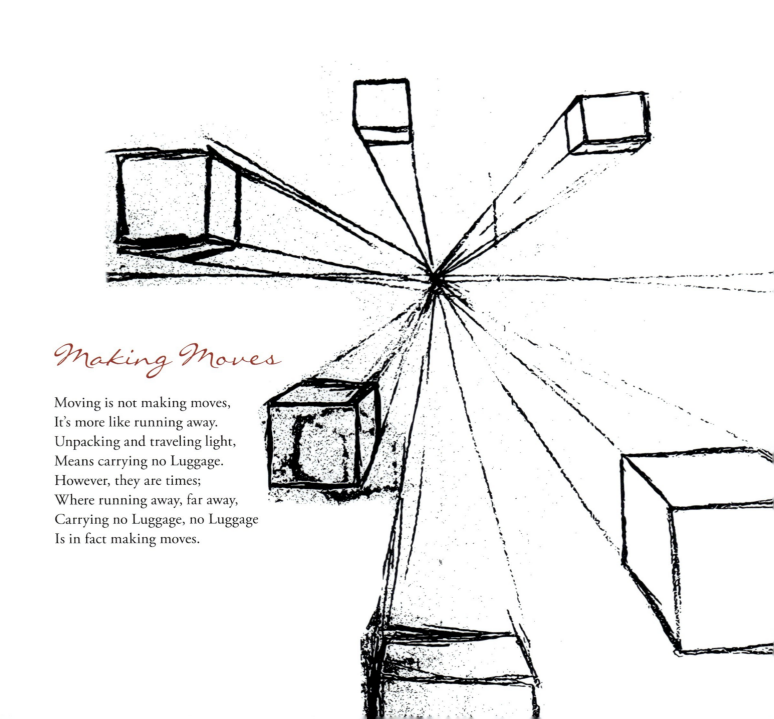

Making Moves

Moving is not making moves,
It's more like running away.
Unpacking and traveling light,
Means carrying no Luggage.
However, they are times;
Where running away, far away,
Carrying no Luggage, no Luggage
Is in fact making moves.

Eyes Forever Closed

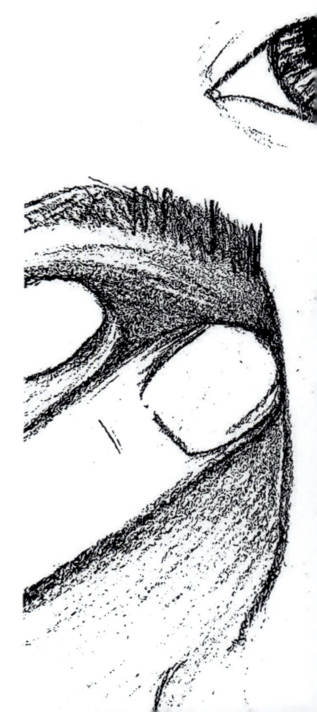

Some don't have a choice;
To live a life of peace.
Scarred and severely burned,
Living with an expired lease.

Blessed for only a day;
Seconds, minutes, hours, or weeks.
Despite not being promised tomorrow,
Their spirit daily, lives and seeks.

Our days has always been numbered;
Young, middle aged, or old.
Born with an expiration date,
No matter what we were told.

Whether we live for long;
Or our days were cut short.
We are all Blessed the same,
Ordained from the highest court.

No matter our complexion;
Whether we speak the same or not.
None of us is better than the next,
Bodies six feet under all still rot.

We all win and lose;
People in life we love.
It's the story and balance of life,
Told by the raven or or told by the dove.

Each day we are Blessed;
To see another day.
Some may beg to differ,
Gone at night as they lay.

Tell them you love them;
Tell them you really care.
You'll regret it that day,
When your voice they no longer can hear.

Wakes and Funerals; occur
Each and every day.
The ones who don't recall,
Are the ones no longer here today.

While your eyes are still open;
Embrace, family, friends, and foes.
Trust me you'll regret it,
When your eyes forever close.

Stranded

I was told I had no ambition;
Was told I'm to complacent.
But, little did she know,
My Blessings was heaven sent.

She thought she knew me;
She didn't really put in the time.
Always tore me to shreds,
Leaving me sour like a lime.

If she only gave me the chance;
Instead of running away.
She would have realized that,
I was the one, the very first day.

So I sit and I wait silently;
As my heart bleeds in pain.
For the lover I once had,
To return from the thunderous rain.

You did say you'll ghost me;
When temperatures raise the flame.
Yet you wonder blindly for a King,
Thinking things will remain the same.

You cut me with your words;
You hurt me to the very core.
Regardless of what was done,
My love for you grows more and more.

Perhaps I'm insanely crazy;
Or mad out of my mind.
Chasing down your being,
As if you didn't leave me behind.

My soul screams for your touch;
Yet you're far from arms reach.
Dying inside slowly,
Left stranded on the beach.

Renew

Shattered into a million pieces;
I am just as broken as you.
Pieces that could never go back,
Until our love is given time to renew.

You're the ghost in the wilderness;
I know is there, but I cannot see.
Slowly driving me insane,
As my mind wonders free.

It wasn't that long ago;
When we first met.
Feelings quickly filled our brim,
Rapidly running us off set.

Heading in different directions;
Yet our hearts have become one.
You were definitely my future wife,
Mother to my daughter and son.

For now it's a distant memory;
That can quickly become true.
Willing to put the pieces back together,
Giving our love the time to renew.

Stuttering Lisp

Some speak perfect and solid,
Chosen words to a crisp.
Me on the other hand,
Got stuck with this stuttering lisp.

They say those that stutter,
Struggle each and every day.
They say those with a lisp,
Have more to really to say.

I stutter and I have a lisp,
So I guess I have tons to say.
Growing up I didn't realize it,
Like I do this very day.

I have been prepared,
Stuttering around with a lisp.
Letting it go on paper,
Struggling with this stuttering lisp.

We Pay

We pay for the transgressions;
Of our ancestors.
Yet drink from the same cup, and
Expect change.

Finally Gone

I'm not ashamed to admit it;
It took me a while to understand.
Thought I really had control, like the
Way one knows the back of their hand.

Spiraling out of control;
Thinking all was really good.
Drowning in all the sorrows,
Masking it the best way I could.

Truth is, I'm barely holding on;
Hanging on by just a thread.
No please don't be concerned,
You'll see me when I am dead.

Laying in the casket like a prop;
Fake tears and words are said.
Spoken by those who were envious,
When alive we didn't even break bread.

All of a sudden you show up; and
I don't even know you're there.
When I was standing next to you,
You didn't even notice or care.

Now that I'm gone and forgotten;
I'm missed more than when I was there.
Why get attached and fall in love,
Only when gone you finally shed that tear.

You think we have the time;
Until all the time is gone.
Believe me I have realized,
That I rather die alone.

You won't be in agony and pain;
If you don't really care for me.
So I stay distant and far away,
Till I disappear like a lost memory.

Leaving no one behind;
You'll be able to move on.
The minute I'm no longer standing,
That day when I am gone.

I rather spend eternity by myself;
Doesn't matter if I am right or wrong.
You have no idea how it feels,
I held on for so very long.

Now willing to give it all up;
I had enough of the lightning and rain.
My next life awaits me,
No more do I care to gain.

Until my eyes finally close;
And my last breathe is done.
You won't shed a tear for me,
Until I am finally gone.

My Words Will Live On

My heart is penned to paper,
I said all that was needed to say.
When my life becomes a vapor,
My words will live on each day.

We Will Meet Again

A few years ago, today.....
You left us with a void.....
No you're not the one to blame.....and
It wasn't something you could avoid.

But, since that day.....
Life hasn't been the same.
I miss you very much.....and
Really wish this was just a game.

If we could trade places.....
You know I definitely would.
You lived a better life.....
Than I most certainly could.

It's always the good ones.....
That's promised a lesser tomorrow.

Then you have ones like me.....
That have to live with grief and sorrow.

I wish I had more to say.....
But you are my baby sister, and
I love you very much.....and
I hope there is a bigger picture.

There's not a day that goes by.....
That you're not in my mind, and
All I can really say.....you
Were the best sis, that anyone can find.

Until, we meet again.....
All I have left to say.
Is that, we will meet again.....and
I'm very hopeful for that day.

DEDICATED TO MY SISTER – Vashti Priscilla Gangadeen - Davis

Printed in the United States
By Bookmasters